YOUR PURPOSE
IS
GREATER
THAN
YOUR TEARS

God's Masterwork

TCM

God's Masterwork LLC
godsmasterwork.com

Your Purpose is Greater Than Your Tears: Finding And Fulfilling God's Unique Calling On Your Life

ISBN (Hardcover): 978-1-7367721-1-9
ISBN (Paperback): 978-1-7367721-3-3

Dr. Terrance L. Caldwell ©2021

TABLE OF CONTENTS

FLOATING DOWN THE RIVER OF LIFE..........................1

GETTING TO KNOW THE CREATOR 11

THE MIGHTY ARCHER 30

THE MAZE RUNNER 38

UNSEEN DANGER 51

DISQUALIFYING YOURSELF 57

THE IN-BETWEEN 72

A DIFFERENT PERSPECTIVE OF FAILURE 80

THE PEOPLE IN YOUR LIFE 85

GO ALONE 102

FINISH THE WORK.. 109

YOUR PURPOSE
IS
GREATER
THAN YOUR
TEARS

Finding and Fulfilling God's Unique
Calling On Your Life

FLOATING DOWN
THE RIVER OF LIFE

Most of us are familiar with the story of Moses. He was born in Egypt, but was a Hebrew by heritage, which made him a part of the slave class. When Moses was only a baby, the king of Egypt ordered that the male children be killed to trim down the numbers of the growing Hebrew population. In order to save his life, Moses's mother put him in a basket and sent him floating down the Nile River, where he was eventually found by Pharaoh's daughter and raised in the palace. Even though he grew up in wealth and privilege, Moses was not numb to the plight of his people. Day by day, he saw them being overworked, beaten, and treated like they were less than human. One day, Moses couldn't take it any longer. He saw one of his fellow Israelites being beaten by an Egyptian taskmaster. The rage that had been building up in his heart reached a breaking point, and Moses killed the Egyptian.

Now a wanted man, he was forced to flee Egypt. He ended up in the country of Midian, where he lived in exile for decades until God spoke to him and revealed that Moses was to be the catalyst by which God would deliver the Hebrews out of Egypt.

It's a classic biblical story, very inspiring and spiritually enlightening if you take the time to read it, but I'd like to do a quick exercise. Let's go back to the point of Moses's story where he saw that slave being beaten by the Egyptian. What if, instead of refusing to sit on his hands any longer while his people suffered, he just sucked it up and went on about his business? What if, from that moment on, he decided there was nothing he could do about the slavery of his people. Yes, it was unfortunate, but God was gracious enough to allow him to escape that fate, so he'd better just make the best of his life and don't try to be a hero.

If Moses had chosen that path, he most likely would have lived out his days in the luxury of the Egyptian palace. He would have taken a wife, had a few children, and been relatively happy. Sure, whenever it got quiet in the palace and he looked upon the slaves, whenever he saw one of his people being mistreated, he would still feel that anger which told him he needed to do something about it. Of course, by then, he would have learned to push those feelings back. "I do hope God frees my people someday," he would think.

The craziest thing about this bizzarro version of Moses is, in all likelihood, we never would have heard of him. Why would we? What would his life have amounted to in the grand scheme of things? He would have been just another random person from history. That, I think you would agree, is a tragedy. What makes it even more tragic is Moses would not have known the kind of greatness he squandered. He would have lived his life thinking that he was just born to be an ordinary person, to just make ends meet for a few decades and then die.

By the grace of God, this version of Moses doesn't exist. Or does he? I think he actually does exist, and we all know him. Of course we know him by different names. He is our friends, our coworkers, or our family members. Many of us see this version of Moses every time we look in the mirror. We go about our daily lives, just doing our best to pay the bills and be happy. God's purpose sits on our hearts, nagging at us every now and then that there's something greater out there for us, but we just brush it aside and keep our minds on our more "realistic" goals. Like baby Moses in the basket, we are simply floating down the river of life, just going with the flow.

Here's a question for you. Do you think God created you to just get a job, work your whole life, maybe raise a few kids, and eventually die? Of course not. That is the life cycle of an ant. You are made in the image of God. If no one has told you before, let me be the first to say there is greatness on the inside of you, and I can prove it.

It's a popular saying that "God doesn't make mistakes," and it is a true statement. You'll never open your Bible and read a passage where it says that He did something by accident. How could He? There are ultimately three reasons a person might make a mistake. In the first place, you might make a mistake due to poor judgement. If you're running late for work and see that you're low on gas, you might decide to skip the gas station and head straight to the office, believing you have enough gas to make it, only to run out of gas because you misjudged the situation. Or, you could make a mistake due to a lack of information. Say you thought your gas tank was full, but end up running out of gas because your gas gauge is broken and you didn't know it. Many times, we make mistakes for lack of control. If you slip on some ice and accidentally spill the drink you're carrying, it is because you lost your balance (i.e. control of your body).

None of these situations can apply to God. God is all-knowing and perfectly wise, so He will never lack information and He will never be a victim of poor judgement. He is always in control of everything He does, so it is impossible for God to do anything by accident. On top of that, it is impossible for God to do anything at random. Randomness requires some lack of information. If you're picking names randomly out of a hat, you're consciously picking a name, but you have deprived yourself of information by hiding the names from yourself. God, being all knowing, cannot hide information from himself. Therefore, he never does anything at random.

So, if God does not make mistakes and never does anything at random, that means one-hundred percent of His actions are done on purpose. I want you to pay close attention to the phrase, "on purpose". When something is done on purpose, just as the words suggest, there is purpose behind it. If you slip and spill your coffee, that was an accident. There was no purpose behind it. If you spill your coffee on purpose because you don't want it anymore, then you spilled it in order to get rid of it. The action had a purpose. This applies to every action you take which isn't a mistake. Every word I type in this book is there for a reason. That is, unless I make a mistake and end up with a typo. Hopefully, you get the point by now. A deliberate action, an action taken on purpose, is an action with a reason behind it. So, if we already know that every action God takes is on purpose, and God created you, then we have to conclude that God created you on purpose. When you were made, there was a specific reason for it. We have already gone through how God raised up Moses to be his people's deliverer, but we see this spelled out even clearer in the Bible when God spoke to the prophet Jerimiah.

"Before I formed you in the womb I knew you, before you were born I set you apart: I appointed you as a prophet to the nations"
Jeremiah 1:5

He told Jeremiah that He knew him and had a purpose ordained for him before he was formed in the womb. Notice that God didn't say, "Now that you're here, I might as well give you something to do." No, He told Jeremiah that he gave him a purpose "before I formed you in the womb." That means Jeremiah had is purpose not just before he was born, but before he was even conceived.

Just like Jeremiah, God gave you an assignment before he formed you in the womb, and He didn't just give you any old purpose because he didn't want you to be bored. When you think about the purpose of a thing, it is always to solve a problem. There was a time when it took too long for people to travel long distances. The invention of the car solved that problem. There was a time when you could not talk to someone who was far away from you. The telephone solved that problem. People don't just invent things because they feel like inventing something, and God doesn't just create people because He has nothing better to do.

Whenever there is a crisis in the world, you always hear someone say, "if God really cares, why doesn't He do something about it?" Well, what if I told you that God does do something about it? When God sees a problem in the world, He creates a solution. If we go back to Moses, we see exactly how God responds to problems.

"Then the LORD said, 'I have surely seen the affliction of my people who are in Egypt and have heard their cry because of their taskmasters. I know their sufferings, and I have come down to deliver them out of the hand of the Egyptians and to bring them up out of that land to a good

and broad land, a land flowing with milk and honey, to the place of the Canaanites, the Hittites, the Amorites, the Perizzites, the Hivites, and the Jebusites. And now, behold, the cry of the people of Israel has come to me, and I have also seen the oppression with which the Egyptians oppress them."

Exodus 3:7-9 NIV

Clearly, God viewed the oppression of the children of Israel as a serious problem. When Moses heard God declaring that He was going to deliver His people out of bondage, he probably got pretty excited. There was all this talk about how He had heard their cry and was going to bring His people into a land flowing with milk and honey. Moses was probably thinking, "Yeah, that's what I'm talking about! Let those Egyptians know they can't mess with your people!" And then God dropped the bomb on him in the following verse.

"Come, I will send you to Pharaoh that you may bring my people, the children of Israel, out of Egypt."

Exodus 3:10

God saw a problem, and so he created a solution. That solution was Moses. Now God sees another problem in the world, and he has created you to solve it. Don't you dare start thinking to yourself that you can't be that important. We'll go over the problem with disqualifying yourself later. For now, you need to understand that you are important to God. Understanding how important you are is the first step toward understanding not only why you are here, but also the reason He is willing to push you (sometimes really hard) into your destiny. The effect your purpose has is a lot bigger than you may think. It isn't just about you. It's not even about your friends and family. The whole world is depending on you—yes, YOU—to get in position.

"For the creation waits in eager expectation for the children of God to be revealed. For the creation was subjected to frustration, not by its own choice, but by the will of the one who subjected it, in hope that creation itself will be liberated from its bondage to decay and brought into the freedom and glory of the children of God"

Romans 8:19-21

When God first created the world, it was covered in darkness (Genesis 1:2). Now, it is covered in darkness again. It is covered in the darkness that thousands of years of sin have caused, and the world is not waiting for God to do something. He already has. It is waiting for the children of God to be revealed. Creation is waiting for the sons and daughters of God to take their rightful place in the purpose that God has prepared for them so that everything can be made right again. Walking in your purpose is a vital part of God's plan to redeem all of creation. This is how important you are to the world. This is how important you are to God. Now whenever your birthday comes around, you have more of a reason to celebrate, because it isn't just the day you happened to be born. It is the day you invaded the earth, and you invaded the earth on a mission from God Himself.

GETTING TO KNOW THE CREATOR

You were put on this planet with a crucial mission from your Creator. You weren't meant to just become an average Joe, floating through life just hoping to get by. By the way, I know God ultimately wants us all to be saved and to be united with him for eternity, but if that was the only reason God created us, we would drop dead a soon as we accept Jesus so we can go straight to Heaven. No, you have a real and vital purpose here on Earth that goes far beyond your kids and your nine-to-five.

That does raise the question though, if God really has this grand purpose for everyone he creates, then why do we see so many average joes floating through life in just the way I described? After all, most of the people we know are nice enough, but they're far from remarkable. If everyone is so special, why don't we see any evidence of it?

First of all, don't be so sure that the people around you aren't remarkable. You would be surprised at the kind of talent you'll find in what seem like average people if you get to know them. Many of them, perhaps more than you think, are fulfilling the purpose God has given them in spectacular fashion, even if you don't find their lives very interesting. The manager at your local McDonalds might have brought more people to Christ than every pastor you've ever met, and you'd never know it.

I will admit though, those people are the exception. The majority of people in the world are average; we couldn't call them "average" if they weren't. They squander their purpose just like the alternate version of Moses I described in the first chapter. Thousands of people die every day not only having gone through life with their mission incomplete, but without ever realizing they even had one. You might be in this boat right now, and there is a reason so many people never realize the reason they were created. It is because they aren't in touch with the Creator.

Imagine for a second that you're a time traveler from 1985. The time travel company you work for has planned for your arrival in 2021 and has given you a phone number to call when you get there so their descendants can find you. You find a small rectangular device laying in the middle of the street. You pick it up, careful not to drop it as it seems to be mostly made of glass, and you find a button on the side that causes the front glass panel to light up. There's a display on it, like a TV, with a bunch of little icons. When you touch the icons, the screen changes, and they seem to be opening programs. Finally, you realize it's a computer! In the future, personal computers are small enough to fit into your pocket. This is incredible. You can't wait to tell your superiors at the time travel company, but you have to find a phone to call them. You look everywhere, but there isn't a payphone in sight. That makes sense. Some people in your time have portable phones. Maybe everyone has those in the future, so there's no need for payphones. You spot a nice young lady waiting at the bus stop and ask if you can borrow her portable phone. She seems hesitant, but you put on your friendliest face and she agrees. To your great surprise, she reaches into her purse and pulls out a rectangular device identical to the one you found upon your arrival. You try to tell her that you need a phone, not a computer, but she looks at you like you're crazy. You look at the little computer in her hand, and the screen is displaying a digital dial pad. It *is* a phone! When you call your time travel company, they explain the concept of smartphones to you. You weren't wrong. It basically is a miniature computer, but it was designed to be a phone, first and foremost. With all the other stuff that it can do, the only way you really know it's a phone is because that is what the manufacturer calls it.

Now, you are way more complex than any smartphone. There are a million things you can do, a million paths you can take in life, and countless experiences that have shaped you into the person you are. It's as if you've been installing apps onto your personality since you were born. You have an education app, a significant other app, a friend app, a sibling app, a child app, a job app, the list goes on. You play so many roles that it's no wonder it's hard to find what you were originally made for. It just looks like another app in your system. The only way you know a smartphone is primarily a phone is because it has "phone" in the name. The maker calls it a phone, so that is what it is. So the question you should ask yourself is, what does the Maker call you?

In the Bible, when God reveals someone's purpose to them, he sometimes changes their name to coincide with their assignment.

When Abram was ninety-nine years old the Lord appeared to Abram and said to him, "I am God Almighty; walk before me, and be blameless, that I may make my covenant between me and you, and may multiply you greatly." Then Abram fell on his face. And God said to him, "Behold, my covenant is with you, and you shall be the father of a multitude of nations. No longer shall your name be called Abram, but your name shall be Abraham, for I have made you the father of a multitude of nations.

Genesis 17:1-5

The name Abraham means "Father of multitudes". God created Abraham to be the father of many nations, and so that is what God called him, even though his father called him Abram. Something similar happened to Abraham's grandson, Jacob.

That night Jacob got up and took his two wives, his two female servants and his eleven sons and crossed the ford of the Jabbok. After he had sent them across the stream, he sent over all his possessions. So Jacob was left alone, and a man wrestled with him till daybreak. When the man saw that he could not overpower him, he touched the socket of

15

Jacob's hip so that his hip was wrenched as he wrestled with the man. Then the man said, "Let me go, for it is day-break." But Jacob replied, "I will not let you go unless you bless me."

The man asked him, "What is your name?"

"Jacob," he answered.

Then the man said, "Your name will no longer be Jacob, but Israel, because you have struggled with God and with humans and have overcome."

Genesis 32:22-28

The name Israel means "Wrestles with God", and his name change did not only reveal who he was but signified a change in his identity. His original name, Jacob, meant "trickster", and he lived up to the name. Jacob had been deceiving people his whole life, but once he wrestled with God, he was able to discover the old trickster, Jacob, was only a mask. That was what everyone had always called him, and so it was what he had always been. It had worked for him, so naturally he came to identify with it. That all changed when he came face to face with God.

One more example of someone whose name was changed to coincide with their purpose was the apostle Peter.

When Jesus came to the region of Caesarea Philippi, he asked his disciples, "Who do people say the Son of Man is?" They replied, "Some say John the Baptist; others say Elijah; and still others, Jeremiah or one of the prophets." "But what about you?" he asked. "Who do you say I am?" Simon Peter answered, "You are the Messiah, the Son of the living God." Jesus replied, "Blessed are you, Simon son of Jonah, for this was not revealed to you by flesh and blood, but by my Father in heaven. And I tell you that you are Peter, and on this rock I will build my church, and the gates of Hades will not overcome it. I will give you the keys of the kingdom of heaven; whatever you bind on earth will be bound in heaven, and whatever you loose on earth will be loosed in heaven."

Matthew 16:13-19

Peter was part of Jesus's inner circle. He was the apostle who asked to come to Jesus when he was walking on the water, and so he got to know Jesus in a way the other disciples didn't. In the same fashion, Abraham received his new identity when he agreed to walk uprightly before God. Are you noticing the pattern yet? These three men received their revelation after they had come closer to God than they had ever been. It did not just come into their minds one day. The only way they were able to hear from God was to make themselves receptive to His voice.

There are several places in the Bible where we are compared to the clay that is used to make pots, with God being the potter. That is because, just like a potter that molds clay into exactly what he wants it to be, God molded you when he created you. Discovering your purpose is a matter of finding out exactly what God wants to make you into. The best way to do this is to get to know the Creator. He and He alone knows why He created you, and He will reveal it to you if you seek after him.

When a potter molds clay, he does so by putting it on a spinning wheel and shaping it with his hands. If the clay isn't on a wheel, it can still be molded to some degree, but it will be lumpy and uneven. No potter can make a perfect shape without a wheel. Needless to say, God is not going to create anything that isn't perfect (we are imperfect now, but that wasn't the case when he created us). That means, if God is the potter and you are the clay, then you need to get on the wheel so that you can be molded into the purpose God created for you.

Getting on the wheel basically means that before you can be used by God, you have to be in a position where you can be shaped and molded by Him. He has a will for your life, but He isn't going to force you into it. It doesn't mean anything to say that we want to be the clay on God's wheel, when our actions show that we'd really prefer to stay stuck in the mud.

If you are not saved, there is no way you are going to be able to fully realize God's plan for your life. First of all, hearing from God on the regular basis means you have to have a relationship with Him. Communion with God requires the Holy Spirit, which you can only receive through Jesus. Even if there was some way you could hear from Him without the Holy Spirit, you are still in your sins if you are not saved. Without the Spirit to convict and guide you, all of your actions are guided by your flesh. You may believe you are a good person even without being saved. You may even be pretty alright, but that doesn't mean you're serving God.

When you accept Jesus as your Lord, that means you are accepting Him as the ruler (that's what the word "lord" means) of your soul. Since accepting your purpose also means submitting to God's plan for your life, and it is not His will that anyone be unsaved, then accepting Jesus is taking the first step toward total submission to God.

Now we have the answer to why so many millions of people are missing out on their purpose. They don't have a relationship with their Creator. They may believe in God. They may have asked Jesus to come into their heart, but having a real relationship is more than just a one-time confession. You have to put in the work. Once you say your wedding vows, you're married, but what's the point of being married if you never spend time together, and only talk to one another when you want something. That isn't a relationship anyone would want, yet it is the relationship too many of us have with God.

Accepting Jesus saves your soul but, again, if being saved was all God wanted you to do, you would have dropped dead as soon as you received Him. A relationship with God allows you to live up to your full potential and discover who you are really meant to be. Since we live in a fallen world, we don't have much control over our flesh. Instead of being molded by God, we are shaped by the environment we grew up in, and the urges that naturally come into our heads. We obey our flesh because we don't know any better, and we believe our flesh is who we really are. Once you begin to obey the Holy Spirit and crucify your flesh, then you can escape from the bondage your flesh has been holding you in. However, you still have to get to know Jesus first. Only then can you become the type of person to whom God will reveal His purpose.

So how do you go about developing the kind of intimate relationship I'm talking about? God has actually been gracious enough to give us a formula which lets us know exactly what traits we need to have to be effective and productive for Him.

For this very reason, make every effort to add to your faith goodness; and to goodness, knowledge; and to knowledge, self-control; and to self-control, perseverance; and to perseverance, godliness; and to godliness, mutual affection; and to mutual affection, love. For if you possess these qualities in increasing measure, they will keep you from being ineffective and unproductive in your knowledge of our Lord Jesus Christ.

2 Peter 1:3-8

Do you see the formula in this passage? It is like a list of ingredients needed to make the perfect meal. We have to add each one to all of the others in order to be effective the way God needs us to be. Let's go over them.

1.   Goodness: If you want God to use you, you have to be good. Now, you might be thinking, "Jesus said there is only one good, and that is God". Yes, and that is exactly the point. That which is not of faith is sin. The only way anything can have even a touch of goodness is if it looks to God. As I've already said several times, you cannot fulfil your purpose, or even really know what it is, until you're making a serious effort to please God above all else.

Goodness also has a more straightforward meaning. It is "good" in the way we usually use the word. "Good" is the opposite of "evil". It goes without saying that God cannot use an evil person. Now if the first thing that comes to your mind is, "Well that doesn't apply to me because I'm not evil," you've already messed up. No, I'm not calling you evil, but if you think there's nothing that God calls evil in your heart, then you should take another look. There is a reason we are told to crucify our flesh, and to take up our cross *daily*. Unless you can honestly say you are a perfect person, then you can always be better. Becoming complicit in your own perceived goodness is one of the worst mistakes you can make. Even if you are really a kind person, that doesn't mean you can't be kinder. Even if you are giving, that doesn't mean you can't be more giving.

Goodness is not a state of being. It is a constant journey toward the perfection God expects from you and the example Jesus set for you.

2. Knowledge: God says his people are destroyed from lack of knowledge (Hosea 4:6), specifically knowledge of His word. We know that our aim should be to please God, and it is impossible to please God without faith. The Bible also says that faith comes by hearing, and hearing by the word of God. Therefore, hearing and doing the word of God is the only way you can please Him. You cannot do the word of God if you don't know what it says.

3. Self-control: The devil does not want you to fulfill the purpose God has for you, and that is why he will use every weapon in his arsenal to keep you from hearing from God. The greatest weapon the devil has is temptation. Don't be surprised if, when you really set your mind on pleasing God, you find yourself facing temptations you never faced before. Don't be surprised if that ex you thought you were over suddenly pops back into your life, or you fall on hard times and might need to do something shady to make a few dollars. If you think you

have a hard time staying on track now, you haven't seen anything yet.

Believe it or not, all this temptation you're going to face is a good thing. As James says, "My brethren, count it all joy when you fall into various trials" (James 1:2). You never know what you can handle until you face it head-on, and once you've conquered temptation you gain the patience to endure the next trial. With every temptation, your self-control will grow. God needs to be able to trust you with your assignment, so He needs to know you won't quit when it gets hard, or that you won't turn your back on him when the devil tries to tempt you.

4. Perseverance: Perseverance or "long suffering" is a lot like self-control in that it involves how you handle yourself when things get hard. The difference between them is self-control involves temptation to sin, which never comes from God (James 1:13). Perseverance, on the other hand, is about staying the course even when it looks like all your hard work is for nothing. When it comes to your purpose, you might have the idea in your head that once you get going, everything is going to be great. You'll finally be satisfied with your lot in life, and you'll be happy. God willing, you will be happy and satisfied,

but that doesn't mean things will always be rainbows and sunshine. There will come days when it feels like you've hit a dead end, or when following God forces you to leave some people in your life behind (we'll discuss that in a later chapter). You might even get to a point where you feel like your passion for your purpose is lost. You might develop a passion for something else and think you've missed the mark and that other thing is your *real* purpose. Perseverance means being able to put all of those thoughts out of your mind and look straight ahead. It means trusting God, even when you feel like his presence is gone from you. The temptation to sin is hard to deal with, but it is nothing compared to the temptation to quit when it seems like you're just spinning your wheels and this whole "purpose" thing isn't quite what you expected.

5.   Godliness: To be godly does not mean to be like God, but to be wholeheartedly dedicated to following Jesus. Godliness in this sense comes when you surrender your own will to the will of Christ, and set your heart on obeying Him. Don't forget, your purpose is not about you. It is about the work God needs you to do. When you have godliness, it means you can say to God, "All of you, and none of me" and mean it. Just like

everything else in the formula, godliness is not a trait, but a journey, because it means killing your flesh every day.

If you are mentally stable and try to hurt yourself, it's not easy to do. That is because you have an instinct for self-preservation. Whether you will it or not, your flesh is programmed to resist being killed. It resists death physically, psychologically, and spiritually. Orienting yourself toward God will mean denying your flesh things it has learned to want and need your whole life and doing things you don't necessarily want to do. It means taking risks that, to your flesh, will seem unnecessary. The only way you can fulfil your purpose is to keep your heart and mind stayed on God.

6. Mutual Affection: So far, I have put a lot of emphasis on how everything needs to be centered on God, and while God is the main person our purpose is for, He is not the only person. God put you on this earth to fulfil a need, and that need is always going to be for someone else. It could be bringing someone to Jesus, helping a business flourish, creating a product that makes life easier for a group of people, the list could go on forever. Whatever your purpose is, in order to perform your

task to the fullest, you must have love for those you are helping, as well as those who are helping you. In fact, you must
have love for people in general. After all, we cannot love God
if we do not love one another (1 John 4:20).

7. Love: Does it even need to be said that love is the most
important part of this formula? Love is the most important of
all virtues (1 Corinthians 13:13); God himself is love (1 John
4:8); love is the reason Jesus emptied himself of his divinity,
suffered, and died for our sins (John 3:16); to love God is the
greatest of all the commandments (Matthew 22:37). Knowing
all this, it should go without saying that there is no point of
even thinking about your purpose if you do not have love in
your heart. That is love for God as well as your neighbor.

Paul makes it very clear that no matter how gifted or vir-
tuous you think you are, it means absolutely nothing if you do
not have love in your heart.

**If I speak in the tongues of men or of angels, but do not
have love, I am only a resounding gong or a clanging cym-
bal. If I have the gift of prophecy and can fathom all mys-
teries and all knowledge, and if I have a faith that can move**

mountains, but do not have love, I am nothing. If I give all I possess to the poor and give over my body to hardship that I may boast, but do not have love, I gain nothing.

1 Corinthians 13:1-3

Hopefully, this formula doesn't discourage you from thinking that you can be used by God. By no means is anyone saying that God cannot use you unless you're a perfect person. We are commanded to be perfect and are supposed to strive for perfection (Matthew 5:48), but God doesn't want you to just sit on your hands until you become some shining example of pure godly perfection. On the contrary, the scripture says that you need to possess all of these things in abundance. In this context, the word "abundance" means to be ever-increasing. You have to have, at least, *some* of every ingredient in the formula and make sure they continue to grow. In that sense, there will never be a time when you've "arrived" spiritually. After all, Jesus was the only perfect person who ever lived, and you'll have a hard time convincing anyone that you are as patient, kind, and loving as he is.

The most important thing is to search your own heart and see which of these you have, and which ones you lack. If you are lacking anything, pray and ask God to help you work on it.

Of the ones you have, work on increasing them. This is how you begin walking in your purpose. Remember, you are an arrow in God's quiver, but an archer needs his arrows to be in good condition. If the arrow is dull, warped, or bent then it cannot fly straight and will miss its target. The word "sin" actually comes from archery. It means to miss the mark. God doesn't miss, so don't be surprised if he chooses to keep you in the quiver until you're ready. So if you find you are lacking any ingredient in the formula, you should rejoice that God hasn't quite thrust you into your purpose yet. He wants you to succeed, and will not send you out until you have all the tools to be successful.

By now, we have biblical proof that God created you with a unique purpose that is vital to His plan for redeeming all of creation. We've also discovered the kind of person God can use, specifically someone who follows the formula He has laid out for us. Now, it is time to get started on fulfilling your purpose. In the next chapter, we'll look at where and how to begin.

THE MIGHTY
ARCHER

My first serious career goal, believe it or not, was to be a professional basketball player. Yes, I wanted to go to the NBA. I played pick-up games and on youth teams as a kid, and I practiced constantly. I would record basketball games and study famous players like Isaiah Thomas of the Detroit Pistons. I didn't hope I could get into the NBA. I *knew* I was going to be a professional basketball player.

I had my whole life planned out in advance. Once I became a rich and famous NBA player (because I planned to be a superstar, not some bench warmer), I would be invited to be a guest on the Arsenio Hall talk show. I figured Janet Jackson would be on the show that same night. We would hit it off and become a power couple.*

This may come as a shock, but that plan didn't quite work out. I knew I was in trouble when Arsenio went off the air. Then I really saw my plans crumble when I didn't make the University of Michigan basketball team. It turns out even college teams are reluctant to put you on the court when you're only 5'9".

Fortunately, I was always taught to have a backup plan. So once I came to grips with the fact that the NBA thing wasn't going to work out, I set my sights on law—or at least law enforcement. I wanted to be either an FBI agent or a lawyer. After four years of college, I heard God tell me not to go to law school. So, FBI it was. I took the entrance exam and I wish I could tell you how I did, but I don't know. I never got the results, just a letter asking me to retake it. If you're keeping count, that's three career goals down the drain.

I kept trying different things until I found myself working in the auto industry. It was a far cry from basketball or law, but I was still happy with the direction my life was headed in. I was a college graduate, which allowed me to make a good living in my new line of work; I had a new car; I had even gotten married at that point. I stopped one day to thank God for the way things were going in my life. I was so thankful for what He had done for me, I told Him that if there was anything He wanted me to do, just let me know. I was not expecting to hear God's response so quickly, and I definitely wasn't expecting the answer I got. As clear as day, I heard God call me to preach.

So I went from professional basketball, to lawyer, to FBI agent, to auto worker, to pastor. These things have almost nothing in common. I can't even say they all led up to me being a pastor, because there's no through line stringing them all together. No, my life up to that point wasn't a journey that eventually led to the destiny I was in search of all along. It was me wandering around randomly trying to find the career that would make me happy. I didn't discover my purpose until I stopped and asked God what would make *Him* happy.

I'm almost willing to bet you've had similar experiences. Even if you were one of the blessed few who knew exactly what you wanted to do from an early age and went on to achieve it, you probably still had to go out and look for the right relationship, the right house, the right friends, the right *something* that would gratify your flesh and make you feel like you've made it in life. For a while, maybe you did feel like you made it. However, I'm going to go out on a limb here and guess it didn't last. Otherwise, you wouldn't be reading this book.

One of the biggest mistakes we make is mistaking our goals for our purpose, but a goal is something you set for yourself. It is something you want to achieve. You do it, and then you move on to your next goal. That is why the goals you set can never replace the purpose God has for your life. A goal has an end point. Once you reach it, it's over. A purpose, on the other hand, is not something you do. It is what you are here for. If your life's goal is to become a millionaire, and your bank account hits seven figures when you're thirty-five, what do you do with the rest of your life? If your purpose is to be a millionaire so that you can help the poor, then that lasts a lifetime.

I say all this because before I get into how to find your purpose, I want to make it plain that if, in looking for your purpose, you're trying to find the ideal career, you're already doing it wrong. Your purpose may become your career, but that isn't true for everyone and you shouldn't expect it to be true for you. Searching for your purpose because you want a career you'll be satisfied with means you are still not asking

God what will make *Him* happy. You're hoping to make yourself happy while passively pleasing God in the process, and that's not how it works. The first step in discovering your specific purpose is understanding that, deep down, we all have the same purpose: to serve God. If God told you right now that your purpose was to leave everything you have behind and preach the gospel in a third world country that hates Christians and will try to kill you, would you say, "Yes Lord," or would you walk away grieved like the rich young ruler when Jesus told him to sell his possessions? Just something to think about.

With all that being said, even though your purpose is not necessarily a career, childhood career aspirations are a good place for you to begin searching for your purpose. When you were asked as a child, "What do you want to be when you grow up?" what was your answer, and why? Maybe you wanted to be a veterinarian because you liked animals, or a soldier because you wanted to fight bad guys, or even a professional athlete because it seemed like an easy way to get rich. Whatever you wanted to be, it was something you wanted before you grew up and life began to happen to you. It was something you wanted when you were at your purest and you didn't worry about how you were going to pay bills, or what your family would think of you. There was simply something inside you that resonated with that path. It was a passion that God gave you, and he put that passion in you to point you toward your purpose.

The Bible says, "As arrows are in the hand of a mighty man; so are the children of the youth" (Psalm 127: 4 KJV). This scripture always puts an image of Robin Hood in my head. He always had a quiver full of arrows on his back, and when he took out an arrow and shot it from his bow, he never missed his target. He always shot straight and accurate. He shot his arrows…wait for it…with purpose. No matter what ver-sion it was, I never saw a depiction of Robin Hood that just whipped out his arrows and shot them willy-nilly all over the place. Robin Hood always hit his targets because he knew ex-actly where he wanted his arrow to land, and how he was going to get it there. Sometimes he would have to bounce it off one or two targets before it reached its destination, but every single arrow had a specific assignment.

As great as Robin Hood was, if I had to put my money on who was a better archer between him and God, I would choose God. He is the mighty man (Exodus 15:3), and we are the ar-rows in his hands. Just like Robin Hood, he gave us a purpose before he drew us back on his bowstring and launched us to the earth. For Jeremiah, it was to be a prophet. For Peter it was to be an apostle. For Abraham, it was to be a father of many nations. For you, it could be that dream you've had since you were a child. Remember, God called Jeremiah when he was a child, and he wasn't the only one. David was only a child when he was anointed to be king of Israel, and Jesus was about his Father's business at the age of twelve. God plants the seeds of purpose within us when we are born, and they can begin to blossom very early on.

As an exercise, try this: List three different life goals you had growing up, and why. Be honest with yourself. If you thought it would be a good idea to pursue a career because you thought it would make you rich, write it down. Even the fact that you were chasing after riches at such a young age could give you insight as to where your passions lie.

After you've written them down, look at your reasons. Not the careers, just the reasons. Now, on a scale of 1 to 10, rate how important that reason is to you now. For example, I wanted to be a basketball player simply because I loved basketball and I wanted to do it professionally. It wasn't complicated. Nowadays, I would rate the importance of actually *playing* basketball lower than I would have when I was in high school. Don't get me wrong, I still love to play it, but it isn't everything to me.

If you look at your reasons and find there are one or two you are still very passionate about, then you should pray and ask God to reveal to you why He gave you this passion, and how you can use it to serve Him. Once you've gotten the answer to that question, you've taken the first step toward discovering your purpose. Of course, this is also the easiest step. Once you discover your passion, you're on your way, but it doesn't mean your purpose is just going to fall into your lap. Now that you know where to begin, it's time to step out and see where God leads you.

THE MAZE RUNNER

If you've ever done a maze on paper, you know how irritating it can be to try and trace your way to the end, only to hit a wall halfway through and have to start over. What's even more irritating than doing a maze on paper is being in one of those giant mazes in a cornfield or made from trimmed bushes, where the walls are too high to see over and you have to navigate your way out.

Getting started on your purpose is a lot like being in a maze. Even if you are sure you have heard from God and know that you're headed toward the purpose He has ordained for you, chances are God has not given you a detailed plan for the future. You can't see the whole maze, just the path in front of you and the walls around you. It can be scary, since you know that once you start on your way, you might run into a dead end and have to go back. In the worst-case scenario, you could end up lost. That fear of hitting a dead end is what blocks many people from going after their purpose. They're waiting to be sure of what path to take before they get started. If you are one of those people, you need to understand that you will never see the whole path. God wants you to trust Him and the plan he has for you. Yes, it might look like there are nothing but walls around you, and the maze feels so huge that you're sure you will get lost, but remember you are not alone.

You have a Helper who sits high above that maze and can see it all. He will guide you, but it wouldn't be any help for him to give you all the steps right at the beginning. If He tells you to go forward, then make a left, take two rights, another left, another left, three more rights, wait a few minutes, turn back, make another right, and so on, the instructions will sound like nonsense to you, because you can't see the whole maze. Likewise, God cannot show you the whole plan for your life. As the Bible says:

"For my thoughts are not your thoughts, neither are your ways my ways," declares the Lord. "As the heavens are higher than the earth, so are my ways higher than your ways and my thoughts than your thoughts.

Isaiah 50:8-9

God has to guide us toward our purpose, step by step, for our own sake. His thoughts are so much higher than ours, that we could not possibly understand the intricacies of His plans. Even if we did, if we saw the trials and tribulations that would come along the way, we might be too afraid to get started, or we might try to alter God's plan so as to make it easier. If we do that, we will never make it to our destination. The Lord is our guide, and he will not steer us wrong, but he will only direct us if we trust in him.

Trust in the Lord with all your heart, And lean not on your own understanding; In all your ways acknowledge Him, And He shall direct your paths.
Proverbs 3:5-6

From the outside looking in, it seems like there are some people who have seen the whole path. They've had a burning desire for as long as they can remember and have gotten a clear revelation from God of precisely what they were supposed to do. They have never had a single doubt, and just seem to be riding God's preordained path on cruise control. Do not be fooled. They have had trials and temptations as well. Their path might have been a little less complicated than yours, or it might have been harder. The last thing you want to do is base your journey on that of someone else. Everyone has to run their own maze, and their journey is between them and God. As is yours. If you're still not sure where to begin, that's okay. It doesn't matter where you begin as much as *that* you begin. God will direct your path if you trust him. If you start off a little crooked, he will correct you.

Not everything you try is going to be exactly what God purposed for you to do. If He has chosen not to reveal your purpose to you just yet, it is either because you aren't ready for that revelation yet, or because you still need to seek him a little more. In either case, you may not know exactly what to do, but you definitely can't sit around and do nothing. At this point, it is important that you start the journey, and let God guide you as you go. In fact, starting the journey may be the only way you *can* really discover your purpose.

There's a story in the Bible in which Jesus was approached by ten lepers who asked him to heal them. Now, there were many different ways Jesus healed people of various diseases. One time he told a paralyzed man to rise up and walk; he put clay on the eyes of a blind man; one woman was healed by touching his clothes. All of these people were healed of their ailments instantly, but Jesus's approach to healing the lepers was different. He told them to show themselves to the priest. The scripture says that they were cleansed "as they went" (Luke 17:14). Those ten lepers approached Jesus, desiring something from him, and he gave it to them. However, they didn't actually see the manifestation until they started the journey.

Imagine what would have happened if they asked Jesus to heal them, and when he told them to show themselves to the priest, they just stood there waiting to be healed before they went. When they saw that they weren't being cleansed, they might have started to complain that Jesus hadn't healed them, when he had, but their healing was just waiting for them on their path to the priest.

It may be that the revelation of your purpose is also on the path, and God is waiting for you to start the journey so he can show it to you. It may even turn out that the thing you decide to do isn't exactly what God planned for you. That's okay. If you are diligently seeking Him, and believe even a little that you are doing His will, He will reward your faith (Hebrews 11:6). After all, it only takes faith the size of a mustard seed to move a mountain. That doesn't necessarily mean that God will make whatever you do work. You may still end up failing, but God will turn even your failures into tools that will help you when you finally are operating according to your purpose.

When Jesus came to the disciples, walking on water, Peter asked Jesus to allow him to come to him on the water if it was really him. Jesus told him to come. Peter briefly walked on water but looked around at the wind and the waves, became afraid, and started to sink. He then called for Jesus to save him, and Jesus pulled him out of the water. You might be tempted to think that Peter failed, but he really didn't. He asked Jesus to bid him to come to him on the water, and Jesus was able to immediately reach out his hand and pull Peter up when Peter called to him. That means Peter actually succeeded in coming to Jesus on the water. More importantly, when he did begin to lose faith, he was smart enough to call on Jesus for help.

Personally, I don't think it is a coincidence that when Jesus later asked the disciples "Who do you say that I am?" Peter was the one who was able to give the correct answer. Walking on water might not have worked out the way Peter hoped, but he was still able to experience Jesus in a way none of the other disciples did. He was only able to have that experience because he was willing to step out and do what seemed impossible.

I had a similar experience. When God told me to start Rock Church, I didn't know the first thing about starting a church. I didn't have a building to hold service, I didn't know how to recruit members; all I knew how to do was obey God. As it turns out, that's more than enough to get started. Remember, God didn't create you and then just assign you some random purpose because He didn't want you to be bored. He saw a problem, and he created you as the solution. That means He isn't just going to leave you to your own devices if you are sincerely trying to obey Him. The Bible says that if we acknowledge him, he will direct our path.

That is why you cannot be afraid to start running through life's maze, even though you can't see the way through it. You have a direct link to someone who can see the whole thing. Even better than that, he's the one who designed the maze in the first place. That means you don't necessarily need to know exactly where you're going. As He's guiding you, there might be times you feel like you're going off course, or even going backwards. That might make you a little nervous, but remember the One directing your path can see things that are invisible to you. All you have to do is start the journey, and let God take care of the rest.

Now I know it's easy to say "just get started," but that isn't much help if you don't know *how* to get started. After all you can't run a maze if you don't even know where the entrance is. Some of us are blessed enough to be told explicitly, by God Himself, what our purpose is. If you haven't had that kind of "burning bush" experience, there are two major clues that can point toward what you were designed to do. You may even discover that you're already doing it.

Clue #1: Look at What Makes You Angry

Anger is often looked at as a bad emotion. It isn't, none of our emotions are. God gave us anger as a means of driving us to solve problems. If a person has wronged you, anger might lead you to stay away from them to avoid being wronged again. If you've angered yourself, then chances are you will not repeat whatever mistake you made. In the same vein, seeing the problem that God created us to solve would naturally make us angry.

When I say look at your anger, I mean think about the things that keep you up at night. Think about something you cannot stand to look at. For example, God hates sin so much that he had to forsake Jesus on the cross, and the earth was covered in darkness for hours. What is it that you hate as much as God hates sin? Personally, it used to really bother me that there were thousands (maybe millions) of people going to church every Sunday, sincerely wanting to serve God, but living below the means of what God really wanted them to have.

The example that comes to mind is a woman who I would see standing at a bus stop every Sunday so she could catch the bus to church. Now, there's nothing wrong with catching the bus. Indeed many churches have busses to bring people who do not have a means of transportation. However, I believe that these kinds of things should be temporary for most people. There's no reason a person who is fully capable of driving a car should have to take the bus to church for years because their circumstances have not improved after hearing the word of God for so long. When I would investigate the reason why people didn't seem to be applying the principles of God to their lives, I came to realize it was because so many people didn't understand the Bible. Many times, the preacher may not have understood what he was reading to the people. Everyone was just going through the motions, believing in Jesus but having no idea how to live the life he really desired for them. This bothered me quite a bit, and it wasn't long before I realized

God's will was for me to teach His word in a way everyone could understand.

If there is something that really makes your blood boil, it is because God wants you to do something about it.

Clue #2: What Are You Doing for Free?

Most of us go to work every day for one reason: money. If you love your job, that's great. Even so, if most people weren't getting paid to do their job every day, they'd probably do something else. Of course, there's nothing wrong with working for money. We all have bills to pay, and many of us have mouths to feed. Imagine, though, if you woke up one morning and you no longer needed money. Every one of your needs is met, and your job is no longer giving out paychecks. Would you still work there? Jesus actually commanded his disciples to think this way when he sent them out.

So do not worry, saying, 'What shall we eat?' or 'What shall we drink?' or 'What shall we wear?' For the pagans run after all these things, and your heavenly Father knows that you need them. But seek first his kingdom and his

righteousness, and all these things will be given to you as well.

Matthew 16: 31-33

What Jesus said to his disciples also goes for us. We do not need to chase money. We are to chase God's Kingdom and his purpose, and we might be surprised to find that we didn't lack anything on our journey toward our destiny (Luke 22:35). It is also important to remember that money isn't the end-all-be-all. At the end of the day, God doesn't care how much money we have. True prosperity is being at peace, and there is no greater peace than knowing that you are doing what you were put on this earth to do.

Now, let's go back to the maze analogy for a moment. Imagine you're walking along what you believe is the right path. Suddenly, you come to a corridor with three paths. You can't see down any of them, so you have to decide which way to go. You consult your guide, and you believe He tells you to go left, so you do. To your surprise, you hit a wall. It turns out that wasn't the direction your guide wanted you to go in. It's a little frustrating, but you turn around and go back the way you came. Now, at least, you know that the way you went wasn't the right way and that you shouldn't go down that path again.

Or, if I may use another analogy, imagine you are playing baseball. You're batting and you see the pitch coming. You know that if you take the swing, you could hit a home run, or the ball might curve and you'll miss, getting a strike. However, if you choose not to swing, you'll still get a strike. Wouldn't it be wise to just take the swing and risk the strike? If you hit a home run, you could win the game. If you miss you'll get the same strike you would have gotten if you didn't swing at all. Even if you get the strike, you still have two more to go. You're not out yet.

I remember in high school taking a summer course called DAPCEP (Detroit Area Pre-College Engineering Program), a summer program to prep students that wanted to go into engineering. I was in the program for two years thinking that I was getting a head start on my future career. After my second year, I realized there was a pretty big barrier between me and my budding career as an engineer. Engineering requires a lot of math and statistics. It took me two years in the program to realize I didn't really like math, and I HATED statistics. So engineering was out. Was I angry then, that I had wasted two of my summers in a program that ultimately did nothing for me?

No, because it did do something for me. It showed me engineering wasn't for me. I took a swing at it, and it just wasn't my pitch.

Situations like these are pretty much bound to happen on your journey to your purpose. There may be something you are really passionate about, and think you want to do. Unless God has already told you not to do it, go for it. Remember, it was Peter's idea to step out and walk on water, not Jesus's. In the same way, if you like to cook and want to open a restaurant, then give it a try. It may turn out that you like to cook, but absolutely hate running a business. Now you know that being a restaurant owner wasn't a part of God's plan. You'll be no worse off because of it. Also, if your aim is to please God then even your mistakes are a blessing.

The Bible says that time and chance happen to us all (Ecclesiastes 9:11). Even with God on our side, we can't escape it. Some things in life are just hit or miss. As long as you're aiming to please God, you will eventually hit the home run that is your purpose. There might be a few misses along the way, but you should dust yourself off and thank God for those misses. They help to teach you more about yourself and your purpose, and that will give you even more focus once you get back on the right path.

UNSEEN DANGER

I would like to tell you that once you get started on your purpose, it's just smooth sailing from there, but that would be a lie. In fact, it is just the opposite. The path to fulfilling your purpose is full of obstacles. Some are small hurdles, and others feel like bottomless pits. They may come from the devil trying to get you to quit, or your flesh trying to resist being killed. The remainder of this book is dedicated to all the obstacles that will be placed in your way. The first of these obstacles might not even look like an obstacle at all, because it is so common and so difficult to see. That is the danger of anchoring yourself in the river of life.

Let's rewind for a minute, back to our example of Moses from the beginning of the book. You'll remember Moses's mother sent him floating down the Nile River in a basket. What the story doesn't record, and what you may not know until you really think about it, is the dangers Moses must have faced while he was floating. Rivers are dangerous places for anyone, especially for a baby. The current could have picked up and tipped the basket over, or some Egyptian boat could have come by the basket and killed the child as Pharaoh had ordered. Not to mention the Nile is full of crocodiles that would have gladly had Moses for a snack.

Moses wouldn't have known any of this, of course. Since he was a baby, he didn't even know he was floating on a river. He only knew that it was dark, he was alone, and maybe that he was moving. He might have gotten knocked around a bit. He probably cried from time to time, but for the most part, he was completely oblivious to the dangers God was protecting him from.

This is pretty much the state we find ourselves in when we're floating down the river of life, as described in chapter one. When we see God working in our lives, making a way out of no way, we're quick to rejoice and give him thanks (as we should), but none of us can really know how many things God protects us from which we don't even see. Life is filled with danger, from demonic attacks to our own poor judgement. This goes especially for when we're just floating through life, oftentimes in our sins. Remember, the wages of sin is death. If you haven't given your life to Christ, or if you lived long enough to give your life to Christ, that is proof positive that God has been keeping you safe. If you've ever driven drunk and wasn't seriously injured or killed, if you've ever had a one-night stand with someone not knowing whether or not they were carrying a disease, if you've ever been rude to a restaurant worker and your food wasn't tampered with, you should thank God. You have no idea what kinds of dangers he has shielded you from.

Why does God do this? Well, because he loves you of course, but it goes beyond that. Keep in mind the river of life is just that, a river. Rivers don't go on forever; they all lead somewhere. The river of life leads toward your purpose, and God doesn't want anything to happen to you while you're still on your way. He doesn't want His plan frustrated by anyone, including you, so he looks out for you as you're floating along the river of life. You may be oblivious to where the river leads, you may not even realize you're on it, but God knows and keeps you safe.

This, however, is not an excuse to be reckless. I have to confess I've tricked you a little. While God does protect us all, He is more tolerant of disobedience and poor choices when we don't know we're making them (Luke 12:48). You now know that many of the seemingly harmless choices you've made only turned out that way because God protected you from them. But since we all have had bad things happen for one reason or another, it's safe to say God doesn't always shield us from everything. God is merciful enough to protect us as much as he does. It's best not to put Him to the test (Deuteronomy 6:16).

Sometimes, though, you might find yourself taking advantage of God's divine protection without even knowing it. Since you can't see the dangers of the river of life, you might get so comfortable with your state of floating through, that you'll give up on the journey altogether. There may be a place along that river that's comfortable, so comfortable in fact that it seems crazy to go on since there's no way it can get any better. Therefore, you throw out an anchor and decide that you've gone far enough along the river of life, and you don't need to reach that destination. Either that or you become convinced that this new comfort zone of yours *is* the destination. While this seems to be a good idea for you, you have no idea what you're really doing by stopping in the middle of the journey.

Christians are not exempt from this state of affairs. In fact, coming to church, accepting Jesus, and holding positions in the ministry are great ways for people to find fulfilment along the river of life and choose not to keep moving forward. Now, this isn't sin and it doesn't make you a bad Christian, but it still means that you are not living up to your full potential, and you are not living the life God intended for you, and this mistake can have far-reaching consequences.

In the Bible, Abraham's father, a man named Terah, found himself travelling to Canaan (the Promised Land) hundreds of years before Moses was even born. Unfortunately, he decided to take a break in the land of Haran. Instead of moving on to his destination, he found a comfortable place along the way, and stayed there for the rest of his life.

Abraham's seed was always supposed to possess the land of Canaan. If Terah had continued his journey, Abraham's children would have been born in the Promised Land, and so the children of Israel would have been there from the beginning. Instead, Terah's descendants were enslaved by the Egyptians, and were forced to fight and die for the land that should have been theirs all along. Instead of being born into the Promised Land, it took them four hundred years to possess it.

When we fail to reach the purpose God has for us, it can make life harder on the people around us and the people that come after us. But, once again, we do these things without re-alizing we're doing them. As a baby, Moses didn't know he was on a river. Likewise, Terah is described as a man who fol-lowed after false gods (Joshua 24:4). He had no idea he was headed to the Promised Land. That is why floating through life without guidance is so dangerous.

You, by the grace of God, don't have Terah's excuse. You know that just because God has blessed you with comfort, it doesn't mean he wants you to stop. He will often give you rest when you are weary, but the last thing you want to do is turn comfort into complacency. If you find yourself having an easy time with everything you do and just coasting along, that doesn't mean God is finished with you and you can just chill for the rest of your life. There is always more work to be done.

DISQUALIFYING YOURSELF

There is another reason why people fail to fulfil their purpose which I haven't addressed, but which needs to be discussed in length. It may be the single biggest obstacle along the path to purpose, and that is the issue of disqualifying oneself. In a previous chapter, I stated that we all start off with dreams of what we will become, but the obstacles life throws at us usually cause us to forget about those dreams and focus on something we deem more "realistic". In principle, there's nothing wrong with setting realistic goals. After all, a goal you can't reach is a waste of time. But then, what is it that makes a goal realistic? There are a lot of factors that go into it, but most of those who shift gears and try to do something more practical only really have one criterion for what constitutes a realistic goal: it has to be small.

People give up on their purpose because they believe they're dreaming too big, that they could never accomplish something as grand as they are imagining. They think that maybe they could if they were richer, or smarter, or younger, or better educated, or any number of qualifications that they set on themselves. There may be a lot of circumstances in which prerequisites like these do have to be met, but not with God's purpose for your life.

God isn't limited to how man believes things should work, and he operates in eternity. That means that while your long-term goals might be five to ten years, his extend forever. Try to think of how someone could possibly carry out a plan as huge as that, and you will understand the reason we can't comprehend God's methods. The mistake people often make when it comes to God's plan for their lives is that they believe it isn't possible simply because it isn't comprehensible.

Since it isn't easy to convince someone that what they think is impossible can actually be done, I think it's best that I look at all of the major reasons people disqualify themselves from their purpose, and then look at the biblical examples of people who used the very same excuses, but were used by God in amazing ways once they surrendered to His plan and let Him work through them.

Age

Age as a disqualifier can go two ways. Those who use it say they cannot fulfil their purpose because they are either too young or too old. This is probably the easiest barrier to overcome because it is all in your head. As the old saying goes, "Age ain't nothin' but a number." When God was planning out destinies at the moment of creation, he wasn't setting age limits on them. It is never too early to get started on what God has put in your heart. It can be too late to start, but that is decided by God, not you. Of all the things that should concern you regarding your destiny, age is the least of them.

In order to see how God feels about age as a disqualifier, we look once again at the prophet Jeremiah. When God told him that he had ordained him to be a prophet, Jeremiah gave an unexpected response.

"Alas, Sovereign LORD," I said, "I do not know how to speak; I am too young."

Jeremiah 1:6

Can you imagine that? God himself spoke to Jeremiah and told him that He wanted to make him the next in a long line of great prophets, one who would speak to the nations on behalf of God. His reaction to this stunning revelation was to make the excuse that he was too young. One has to wonder what he was expecting God to do with that information, as if He didn't already know Jeremiah's age. God's response went as follows:

But the Lord said to me, "Do not say, 'I am too young'. You must go to everyone I send you to and say whatever I command you. Do not be afraid of them, for I am with you and will rescue you," declares the Lord. Then the Lord reached out his hand and touched my mouth and said to me, "I have put my words in your mouth. See, today I appoint you over nations and kingdoms to uproot and tear down, to destroy and overthrow, to build and to plant."

Notice that God's first reaction to Jeremiah's disqualifying himself was to tell him not to say what he'd just said. This is important, because it is a lesson we all need to know about this and all other disqualifiers. Regardless of what we believe, our words carry weight in the spiritual realm and in our own minds (Proverbs 18:21). The things we say affect us in more ways than we would like to believe, and right then, those words were holding Jeremiah back from his destiny and God wasn't having it. Whatever you might be saying or even thinking that disqualifies you from your purpose, make every effort to put it out of your mind.

Also notice the second thing God did was reach out and touch Jeremiah's mouth, and then told Jeremiah that He had put His words into his mouth. That is to say, He touched the very area where Jeremiah was weakest and felt he wouldn't be useful. This is another lesson we can all take from God's interaction with Jeremiah. God is not going to give you a task without providing you with the tools to carry it out. If the area he is calling you to seems like one where you are particularly weak, then you should rejoice, because the Bible says that God's strength is made perfect in our weakness (2 Corinthians 12:9). That means God works best in the areas where we work worst, because we have no choice but to surrender to the will of God and let Him work in us, instead of trying to use our own strength/skills/intelligence to get the job done.

If you're ever thinking that you're too old or too young to do what God is calling you to do just remember this: God is omniscient. He knows how old you are.

Credentials

I can't say how many people I've spoken to who have great God-given ideas, but will not step out and attempt to pursue them because they feel they don't have enough education or experience. What those who feel they don't have the credentials for their purpose fail to understand is that the concept of having credentials is entirely manmade and irrelevant to God. Growing up in a society where nothing is more important than having a degree, except maybe having experience to go along with it, we have been brainwashed into thinking God works the same way our workforce does. Surprise, he doesn't.

There is a big difference between God and an employer or a lender. When a job wants a new employee, they look for the best candidate and hire them. When a lender is judging who they will give money to, they pick the best candidate. When God needs a purpose fulfilled, he *creates* the best candidate! You may not have been born with a Ph.D., but you were born in just the right place, at just the right time, to have the right knowledge and experiences to drive you to your purpose. For an example of this, let's look to Moses again. When God told Moses that he was to be the one to deliver the children of Israel out of Egypt, Moses actually made several excuses for why that wouldn't work, but only one of those excuses involved a shortcoming on his part. Moses tried to bring up his lack of eloquence.

But Moses said to the Lord, "Oh, my Lord, I am not eloquent, either in the past or since you have spoken to your servant, but I am slow of speech and of tongue."
Exodus 4:10

Once again, God gives a no-nonsense response.

Then the Lord said to him, "Who has made man's mouth? Who makes him mute, or deaf, or seeing, or blind? Is it not I, the Lord? Now therefore go, and I will be with your mouth and teach you what you shall speak."
Exodus 4:11-12 ESV

As with Jeremiah, God reminded Moses that he wasn't going to be in it by himself. God isn't that terrible partner we all got stuck with while doing group projects in school, the one who abandons the group at the beginning of the project and leaves everyone else to do the work without him. God is more like the smart kid who will do most of the work as long as you show up and put your name on the paper.

God also reminded Moses that it was He who made man's mouth. That specific area where Moses said he wasn't qualified, is something that God created. Do you feel that God is calling you to take a certain job, but you don't have the proper degree? Ask yourself, who made college degrees? Who made classes? Who made the human brain? Was it not God? God knows what credentials you do and do not have. If he is putting you in a place where credentials are required either by man or by necessity, he will either give you a way to bypass it or provide you a way to get the credentials you need. I can attest to this myself.

When I started Rock Church, services were held in the basement of a community center. Band rehearsals and church meetings were held at the homes of members. As membership would grow, I knew that I would eventually have to expand into an actual church building. Unfortunately when I went to apply for a loan, I ran into a problem: I didn't have the credentials. Notice I didn't say I didn't have the money. I'd saved up enough money for a down payment and then some. The banks I'd gone to were actually impressed with the amount we were willing to put down. But money wasn't enough. The problem was that my church was under three years old. Rock Church was open and growing rapidly, but that didn't stop them from saying we hadn't been around long enough to be considered well-established enough to buy a building.

You can imagine how frustrating it was to hit a roadblock that I could do nothing about. If we needed more church members, we could have recruited more members. If we needed more money, we could have gotten more money. But how could I make my church…older? I could have just waited, of course, but that would have meant continuing to jam my congregation into that small room we would meet in every Sunday. I knew that that was not God's plan for Rock Church, so I'd get home from work, shower, put on a suit, and head off to another bank every day. I knew *someone* had to see what we were doing and believe in it more than they believed in their risk assessments. After all, Rock Church was God's idea to begin with. He wanted us to have a permanent home, and so He would provide one. Lo and behold, He did.

So guess which bank finally approved us. None! Every single bank I set foot in denied me. My church was able to find a place of worship due to a series of events I could never have seen coming.

The realtor I had been working with told me that there was a building he wanted to show me, and asked me to meet him there. I did meet him there, but we weren't able to look at the building. The seller was supposed to meet us there so I could take a look at it, but he didn't bother to show up. While I was waiting in my car, the realtor came to talk to me. He apologized for the inconvenience, but he told me there was another building that had just come on the market that I might be interested in. I figured it wouldn't hurt, so I went with him to look at the building. It turned out to be pretty nice. It was a decent size, and was already a church building so we wouldn't have to do much renovating. It looked like a good place to finally put my church, so I spoke with the pastor of the church that was occupying the building, and he seemed to be on board. All he had to do was talk to his bishop, and I would be all set.

Once again, I didn't have the credentials. The church that had occupied the building was of a particular denomination, and the bishop wanted to keep the church with that denomination. Our ministry is nondenominational. But the pastor advocated for me, telling his bishop that there was something about me that made him feel like selling the building to me was the right move. By the grace of God, he convinced the bishop to sell me the building anyway. Praise God, Hallelujah, but wait, we were still missing a credential. I had the down payment in hand, but the banks didn't sense that same "something" that the pastor did. I still needed a loan.

Bishop I.V. Hilliard once said, "when your heart is right towards God, He will raise up people to help you." Praise God that through my agent, I met a private investor who was willing to finance the building for me, and we pay him. This guy didn't know me from Adam. The risk he took for me was incredible. He told my agent he believed in me and, like the pastor from before, there was something he liked about me. Praise God for favor.

Now, what if I had just decided that I was wrong and it wasn't really God's will for me to have a building at the time. What if I had waited another year? I probably would have never met that man, and would have probably had to move into a building of much poorer quality than the one I was in. The reason that didn't happen is because I trusted God and I remembered that he was bigger than a risk assessment.

There is one more thing I want to address when it comes to this story. The private investor asked to see my books. I did not have to ask him for a few weeks or months to put something together. I already had my documents ready to go. Please understand, when God tells you to do something, prepare for it right then because you don't know when you will need to use it. Even though in that particular season of my life, I didn't have the credentials, I had things in order as if I did.

Fear of What's Ahead

Some people (I could even say most people) are simply afraid of what the future holds. While they are not fully satisfied with their circumstances, their fear of making things worse prevents them from fulfilling God's plan for their lives.

There are quite a few examples of this kind of fear in the Bible, but it shows most obviously in the words of the scouts Moses sent to spy out the Promised Land before the Israelites went in to claim it.

And they brought up an evil report of the land which they had searched unto the children of Israel, saying, The land, through which we have gone to search it, is a land that eateth up the inhabitants thereof; and all the people that we saw in it are men of a great stature. And there we saw

the giants, the sons of Anak, which come of the giants: and we were in our own sight as grasshoppers, and so we were in their sight.

Numbers 13:32-33

There's so much to take from this passage in regards to disqualifying yourself from your purpose. God had promised the land of Canaan to the Israelites long before this passage, and the time to claim what was promised to them had finally come, but then something happened to the scouts which has happened to so many of us: They got a glimpse of what was ahead, and they lost faith.

Think about a time when you truly believed something was for you, even ordained by God, and was fully prepared to get it. Then you saw how much work it would take, or how expensive it was, or the level of competition you had, so you gave up without even trying. This is exactly what happened to the scouts. They were eager to possess the land until they saw that the battle might not be the clean sweep they wanted it to be. They saw the sons of Anak and became afraid that maybe it wouldn't work out after all, in spite of what God had already told them.

The worst part, however, is what they said at the end of the passage. They said that they became grasshoppers in their own sight, and so they were in the sight of the sons of Anak. Pay close attention to the order in which they said those words. They were grasshoppers in their own sight *then* they became grasshoppers in the sight of their enemies. When you look at what the future holds and become afraid of it, your thoughts turn your fears into reality. That is why it is important to always remember that what you are doing as been ordained by God. If God is on your side, there is literally nothing in the world that can stop you (Romans 8:31).

Money

The last disqualifier is probably the main reason people disqualify themselves, and that is lack of money. People feel that they need funding to get started. I beg to differ. You need a word from God to get started. The Bible says write the vision and make it plain. Then it says that the people that read the vision will run with it. They will bring the resources, they will bring fresh ideas, they will help bring it to pass. Where people mess up is that they get the vision and try to run with it by themselves.

In corporate America, corporations don't always use their own money. They have board meetings and presentations in front of investors. The corporation has a vision, and they present it to the investors. The investors like what they see and they reach in their pockets to fund the corporation's vision. Don't be discouraged because you don't have the money. You need to be writing the vision right now and making it plain.

People tend to feel that they need all of the money right now, or the customers right now, etc. Remember the story of the ten lepers who desired to be healed by Jesus. Jesus told them to go and show themselves to the priest, and they were cleansed as they went. The cleansing did not happen immediately when Jesus said it, but by them being obedient. As they were going, as they were in route, as they were on the journey, healing started taking place. What you need may not be in front of you right now, but as you start the journey, what you need will start showing up.

Don't forget, when we pray the Lord's Prayer, we say, "give us this day our daily bread", meaning God will give you what you need for that day! You are frustrated about what you need for next month and you just need what God has for you for today. He will make sure you have what you need for tomorrow.

THE IN-BETWEEN

O nce you've successfully started the journey toward your purpose, you will find yourself in one of two situations. You will either be waiting to hear from God concerning what your purpose is, or you will know what your purpose is and will find yourself waiting for God to reveal to you what you need to do next in order to move closer to fulfilling your purpose. You might find yourself in the second situation multiple times. The question then is, what should you do while you're waiting? God definitely doesn't want you to just sit on your hands, waiting for a burning bush to show up. The best thing to do in this situation is to continue to serve God. If you do not know how you're supposed to serve God when it comes to your assignment, it is probably in your best interest to help someone else with their assignment.

So if you have not been trustworthy in handling worldly wealth, who will trust you with true riches? And if you have not been trustworthy with someone else's property, who will give you property of your own?

Luke 16:11-12

If you want what is your own, the way to get it is to be faithful over what is not yours. This shouldn't be a hard principle to understand, especially if you are a parent. There might be a situation in which your child wants something new, but you give them something that belonged to you or one of their older siblings instead. If they didn't take care of it, would you still spend your hard-earned money on a brand new one? Of course not. It would only be a waste of money for them to destroy something that is brand new. If they don't destroy it, that's even worse, shows that they only value it because it is new, in which case they do not deserve it.

The same principle applies to your purpose. If you're waiting for God to reveal your purpose to you, you're probably already helping someone else with their purpose in some way. You're working at someone's business, serving in someone's church, or volunteering with someone's organization. If you're not doing any of those things, then now is a good time to start. If you are doing these things, but aren't doing them with all your heart, then now is a good time to start doing that too.

Let's say for example that you're serving as an usher at your church. Pastoring the church is your pastor's purpose, and God is watching everything you do. If you're constantly doing your job with a bad attitude, or doing the bare minimum, then you're probably going to treat your own assignment the same way.

That's not true, you think. You might be slacking when it comes to someone else's assignment that you're just helping with, but you would never do that when it comes to your own purpose. It's what you were made for, so you would put your heart and soul into it. If this is your frame of mind, then you're like the child who only values their parent's gift because it is new. If you're planning on giving it your all when you finally receive your assignment, but you're not giving it your all right now, you need to look at yourself and make sure you really want to serve God, or if you just want to discover your purpose because you think it will do something for you. If you just want it for yourself, then you are self-serving and God cannot use you. If you want to do it for God, then you should remember that you should be doing *everything* for God. If God has called you to be an author, but you're currently an usher, then you should be the greatest usher the world has ever seen. It is only when God sees that He can trust you to be faithful in something that is not your purpose, that he will reveal your actual purpose to you.

Here's another example. Have you ever had to pick someone up for work, church, or any kind of appointment. You call before you leave the house to let them know you're on your way and to be ready when you get there, only to get to their house and sit in the driveway for half an hour because they aren't ready. It's beyond frustrating, and you might even tell yourself, "If they don't come out in the next five minutes, I'm leaving." No one likes being put in that situation, so you shouldn't put God in that situation.

If you're waiting for him to show up in your life, one of the worst things you can do is just sit around until he gets there. When God does finally show up, He wants to see that you're working.

It will be good for that servant whose master finds him doing so when he returns.
Matthew 24:43

The principle of faithfulness over another person's assignment is one that has been proven to work. One person it worked for was David. When David first appears in the scriptures, he is taking care of his father's sheep. He eventually tells two stories to Saul that show how serious he was when it came to the sheep.

But David said to Saul, "Your servant has been keeping his father's sheep. When a lion or a bear came and carried off a sheep from the flock, I went after it, struck it and rescued the sheep from its mouth. When it turned on me, I seized it by its hair, struck it and killed it.

1 Samuel 17:34-35

David was only fifteen years old when he fought Goliath[*], and these events happened before that. Even though he was only a boy, David was willing to fight two animals that could have easily killed him in order to keep his father's sheep safe. The sheep weren't even his, but his faithfulness to his father and the assignment he had been given was just that powerful. It should not have come as much of a surprise then that, when

---

[*] This is an estimate based on the minimum age requirement to fight for Israel (20), and the fact that only three of David's six brothers fought against the Philistines. Assuming the other brothers didn't fight because they weren't old enough, that would have put David at around 15 years of age or younger.

Samuel came to anoint the next king of Israel, David was tending to the sheep. When it came time to receive his purpose, he was found being faithful.

David isn't the only person who benefited from faithfulness. This is a subject on which I can speak from experience. Before I was a pastor, I served in my father's church, and not always as an associate minister. I was a drummer, a deacon, a youth pastor; if you can name a position, chances are I did it. And it wasn't all before I knew God was calling me to be a pastor. Once God revealed my purpose to me, that didn't stop me from going wherever I was needed, because receiving your purpose isn't an automatic ticket to stop helping someone else with theirs.

The in-between is also a time for preparation. You should be doing research, attending conferences, and reading books on where you are getting ready to go. Preparation is the key. You should start preparing as if it's time for you to do it. People tend to say that if they had the money there are things they would do. I'm saying that you should be so prepared that when the money shows up, you will just have to sign the check. Most people don't really prepare themselves because they are waiting on the money to show up. Right now you should have everything in place that if I told you I have the money that you need, then this project should be ready for implementation.

I recall a friend of mine wanted to start a company, and he wanted me to invest in it. He presented his idea to me, and I liked it. I was ready to write the check then and there. When I took out my check book and asked him the name of the business account I was making it out to, he informed me that the business did not have a checking account and I would have to make the check out to him. Well, I decided not to do that because I felt he was not ready to do business. You're asking me to do business with you and you can't even receive the funding that you need. This was several years ago and he is still struggling with the business. As someone that was ready to invest in his company, I felt I would not be a good steward if I invested in someone that was not prepared.

When you get a new job, your supervisors don't just throw you into the work without training you. If they do, it is because they have assumed you got your training elsewhere. God treats us the same way when it comes to the job he has for us. You can't be effective in your purpose if you have no idea how to do what God wants you to do. That is why the Bible says not to despise small beginnings. Something might seem like wasting time to us, but God is using every little experience as something that will come in handy in the future. If it doesn't look like what God said, then trust that He is using the experience to develop you. Whatever you do, make sure you don't complain, because it will only set you back. Make sure you work diligently in everything you do, and keep your eyes open for the lessons God wants you to learn. Until you learn them, God will not advance you.

A DIFFERENT
PERSPECTIVE OF
FAILURE

We want to be successful in whatever we do. God, as long as we are serving him, wants us to be successful as well. In the natural, though, this wanting to succeed all the time can transform into a need to always succeed, and that is when we run into one of the hindrances to fulfilling the purpose God has for us, failure. No, I don't mean because people try to fulfill God's purpose and then fail. I mean after a failure or two, far too many people will throw up their hands and say, "This must not be what God wanted me to do," and give up. Of course when they say, "This must not be what God wanted me to do," what they really mean is, "If this was really what God wanted me to do, it would be easier, so I give up."

If you're planning on walking in God's purpose for your life, or if you've already begun the journey, let me give you a heads up. You are going to fail. Are you going to fail at your purpose? No, if you follow God, He will never allow that to happen. What I'm saying is you will enter into something with certain expectations. Maybe you'll get into a partnership with someone expecting the work to be easier, or you'll implement a new idea expecting everyone to love it. Then your partner bails on you or turns out to be incompetent, or your new idea is a flop and everyone hates it.

Sometimes, it will be easier to just brush off that particular failure and move on to the next thing. Some failures, however, will be devastating. They might be so bad as to seriously harm you financially, socially, emotionally, or all of the above. Brutal failures of this nature often come when we are putting too much of ourselves into our purpose, and not enough God. Once you begin successfully operating in your purpose, it is easy to start feeling like your success is because of you. You think you're the one with all the great ideas and sharp instincts. Everything you touch turns to gold, so maybe you'll try this one thing. No need to pray about it. God has been with you all this time. Then, before you know it, it all comes crashing down around you. You wonder, if this was really what God wanted you to do, then why would He allow something so devastating to happen to something He ordained?

The answer is simple, of course. He allowed it to happen in order to humble you. Remember, you are only successfully fulfilling your purpose when you are always looking to God for guidance. The Bible says to acknowledge Him in all your ways and he will direct your path. Notice it doesn't say some of your ways or most of your ways. It doesn't say acknowledge him in ninety-nine percent of your ways. You must acknowledge him in ALL of your ways, and he will direct your path.

Moses was so close to God that they spoke face to face. Yet and still, when Moses let his emotions get the best of him and failed to do things God's way, not even he was let off the hook. God forbid your punishment be as severe as his, but I wouldn't risk it if I were you.

So if you find yourself frustrated by failure, the first thing you should do is retrace your steps. Did you make a wrong turn? Did you start doubting? Did you miss something God told you to do? Did you skip a step by being in a hurry? Did you cancel a step because you thought that it was not needed? Find where you went wrong and get back on track.

Now, failures that result from our own errors will hurt, but they are ultimately understandable. But what about when you do acknowledge him, when you know without a shadow of a doubt that you heard from God, and things still go sideways? The Bible says that the steps of a good man are ordered by the Lord. So if God is ordering your steps, why would He lead you to failure? That's an easy answer: He wouldn't. God does not, cannot, fail. If you heard from God and things did not go quite the way you expected, there could be two reasons for it.

It could be that God has a bigger plan that you simply cannot see yet. Remember, God was with Joseph in Potiphar's house. He served God and Potiphar faithfully, and did not give in when Potiphar's wife tried to tempt him. What did Joseph get in return? Two years of prison. If that doesn't look like failure, I don't know what else you can call it. That must have been agony for Joseph, locked up for so long for something he didn't do. However, what was agony to Joseph was a setup to God. While he was in prison, he met two men and interpreted their dreams. One of those men passed the word of Joseph's gifts to pharaoh, and that was what took Joseph from being a prisoner to being the second most powerful person in Egypt.

If you know you heard from God, trust Him, even in what looks like failure. Remember, He sees the whole picture while you only see a part.

This is why it is important to have a relationship with God and to be in constant communication with Him so that you can clearly hear His voice. If you only think you heard from God, you'll have no way of knowing if your failure is due to a mistake on your part, or if it is all part of God's plan for you.

No matter how you look at it, no failure is truly a failure (except a failure to obey God). I have reached a place in life where for me, I have changed my perspective on failure. I don't fail anymore. If whatever I'm doing does not work, I just view it as "I learned that this particular way does not work". Basically, I learned a lesson from this. It's not failure if you learned something from it.

THE PEOPLE IN
YOUR LIFE

There's a reason the Bible warns us not to put our confidence in man (Psalms 146:3). No one is perfect, and no matter how good a person is, they will eventually let you down. Everyone has flaws, everyone makes mistakes, and in the end, everyone dies. That is why when it comes to purpose, there ultimately is no buddy plan. God will put people in your life to help fulfill your purpose, but at the end of the day, you will eventually have to go it alone.

That is why it is important to recognize the people in your life and the role they will play in helping you to fulfil God's purpose. Not everyone is meant to be there forever, but you should thank God for everyone he sends to aid you, even if you wished they could have stayed in your life longer.

Letting go of the people who aren't meant to come with you is one of the hardest parts of fulfilling your God-given purpose. When God created you, He was specific in your development and your path. As much as you might love for your close friends to go with you, you must realize that everyone is not going where you are going. As you walk the path God has ordained for you, you will see your circle begin to get smaller.

Please understand, I'm not saying your old friends can't be there for you. I'm not necessarily saying you have to cut them off, but you have to listen to God when He is trying to broaden your horizons. He is trying to network you; He is trying to push you further. That is why He begins to put different people in your life to serve specific purposes. You need to be able to recognize these people and the purpose they are meant to serve for you. In order to better understand those people and purposes, we will look at Jesus and the people who came into his life at various stages in his ministry, and what their ultimate purpose was.

Laborers

It is a common misconception that Jesus only had twelve disciples. Yes, he did have the main Twelve, who are named in the gospels, eleven of whom went on to become the Twelve Apostles (we'll get to them later), but Jesus actually had many disciples. At one point, Luke records that he appointed seventy-two disciples to go ahead of him and preach the gospel.

After this the Lord appointed seventy-two others and sent them on ahead of him, two by two, into every town and place where he himself was about to go. And he said to them, "The harvest is plentiful, but the laborers are few. Therefore pray earnestly to the Lord of the harvest to send out laborers into his harvest.

Luke 10:1-2

These seventy-two disciples were laborers, people whom Jesus trusted to take his ministry to places he could not go. It wasn't that he couldn't go to these places because he wasn't allowed, or because he had no way of getting there. He simply needed to take his message of the Kingdom to as many people as possible, and he couldn't be in two places at once. That is what he meant when he said, "The harvest is plentiful, but the laborers are few." If he told the seventy-two he sent to pray that God send even more laborers, imagine if Jesus had tried to do it all himself? It would have been impossible, and some people who needed to hear the gospel would have missed it.

When you begin to walk in your purpose, you might find yourself getting overwhelmed with the amount of work that God wants you to do. If you are doing your best and it feels like too much, it might not be because you're not good enough. It could be that you need help, and that is what laborers are for. There will be people in your life who are put there to help you reach places and people you may not have been able to reach on your own. Laborers could be friends or family members, especially when you're starting out. Depending on what your purpose is, laborers could also be employees or volunteers.

Other than the work he gave them to do, the Bible does not make any mention of Jesus's relationship with these seventy-two disciples. He did not, for example, give them the keys to the Kingdom like Peter. He did not show them his transfigured body like James and John. He only sent them to do the work. That doesn't mean these people were unimportant or disposable. Again, they helped Jesus get his message out to people he would not have otherwise reached. However, he did not give them more responsibility than they could handle.

When you have laborers in your life, be sure to maintain a healthy distance with them, for their sake as well as yours.

There are far too many good working relationships that end up ruined because someone tried to deepen the relationship. That is when personality conflicts begin to affect the vision because one of your laborers feels like things could be done better. It is when a laborer might get so invested in your purpose, that they don't go on to fulfil their own because they are afraid you will feel betrayed if they leave you. Laborers are, almost by definition, temporary workers. Even if they help you for years, your purpose is only a small part of their life, and they must be allowed to fulfil their own purpose.

Vision Partners

After the seventy-two, there were the Twelve Disciples we all know and love. These twelve men walked side by side with Jesus, leaving their own families and careers behind to follow him from town to town, from city to city, as he went about his Father's business of announcing the coming Kingdom of God on Earth. They were witnesses to his most profound teachings, and were sometimes victims of his harshest rebukes. They ate with him, laughed with him, and were among the first to see him when he rose from the dead. In short, they were his friends.

The Twelve were more than just Jesus's friends though. They were intimately connected with his purpose. Jesus's mission was to defeat sin and death by dying on the cross, and then establish the Kingdom of God on Earth. A lot of that kingdom establishing work was put on the disciples after Jesus ascended to Heaven. He had already begun to make disciples, but it was up to the Twelve to establish the Church and make disciples of the whole world. They gained their purpose through him.

The difference between laborers and vision partners is laborers are only there to help you fulfil your purpose. If you don't bother to fulfil your purpose, it doesn't really have much of an effect on them. Vision partners, on the other hand, are people whose purpose is directly connected with yours. If Jesus's death had not established the Kingdom, there would have been no apostles because there would have been no need for the Church.

God will send people to you who will be connected to you in this way. They are people who will need to either learn from you, as the disciples learned from Jesus, or who share a common purpose with you. They will probably be your friends, not because you happened to grow up in the same neighborhood, or because you went to the same school, or even because you share similar interests (though all of these things might be true). The Holy Spirit will bring you together because of the connected nature of your purpose.

Now, the important thing to remember about vision partners is that just because your purposes are connected doesn't mean your purposes are the same. There will be places where your paths diverge, and the worst thing you can do is try to pull them back on the path you're on because you're so used to them being there.

For example, if your purpose is to establish a non-profit that helps feed the homeless, you will attract donors. In fact, you might attract someone who God has purposed to be a philanthropist, to provide funding for Kingdom projects. You two might be vision partners in that they are your biggest donor, and provide a huge percentage of the funding for your organization. One day, your partner comes to you and says he will be donating to a new startup, one that seems to need the money more than you do. But you've already made plans for the following year, and it includes his monthly donations. Without that funding, all of your plans will go down the drain. You feel hurt and betrayed that your friend, someone who you know God put in your life to help you, has left you high and dry.

Of course, they haven't left you high and dry. You made the mistake of putting your confidence in man, which is an easy mistake to make when it comes to dealing with Vision Partners (and with the people we'll talk about in the next section). Nine times out of ten, you become friends with your vision partners, you start to feel like your purpose is a joint venture. Then the line that connects you becomes your lifeline, which you cannot let happen. God is your only lifeline, and if you ever begin to cling to anyone else, you better believe He's going to cut that line.

When Vision Partners begin to drift away, don't cling to them. Let them go. If you can, maintain your friendship, but never try to make them believe that your purpose and theirs are so closely tied together that they're betraying you or, even worse, betraying God by moving in a new direction. It might be the case that your purpose and theirs are intertwined this way, but that is up to God to decide, not you.

Confidants

One thing you will begin to notice about your Vision Partners is that some will be closer to you than others. This might be because some Vision Partners will be your family members or your spouse (your spouse is almost certainly going to fall into one of these categories, and it will most likely be this one). Even if they are not related to you, you will notice that your connection with them is so intimate, it will almost feel like you're related. They will be people you feel like you can talk to, people with whom you can share your deepest secrets without fear of judgement. They are people who will pray with you and for you, who you will be able to lean on when the weight of your purpose feels too heavy to bear.

These people are your confidants. Jesus had three of them: Peter, James, and John. They are commonly referred to as Jesus's "inner circle" because they were closer to him than the other disciples, the ones he trusted the most. The bond Jesus had with his inner circle is shown in the story of him raising Jairus's daughter from the dead.

Then came one of the rulers of the synagogue, Jairus by name, and seeing him, he fell at his feet and implored him earnestly, saying, "My little daughter is at the point of death. Come and lay your hands on her, so that she may be made well and live." And he went with him.

Jesus said to the ruler of the synagogue, "Do not fear, only believe." And he allowed no one to follow him except Peter and James and John the brother of James. They came to the house of the ruler of the synagogue, and Jesus saw a commotion, people weeping and wailing loudly. And when he had entered, he said to them, "Why are you making a commotion and weeping? The child is not dead but sleeping." And they laughed at him. But he put them all outside and took the child's father and mother and those who were with him and went in where the child was. Taking her by the hand he said to her, "Talitha cumi," which means, "Little girl, I say to you, arise." And immediately the girl got up and began walking (for she was twelve years of age), and they were immediately overcome with amazement. And he strictly charged them that no one should know this, and told them to give her something to eat.

Mark 5:22-24; 5:36-43 ESV

Jesus performed miracles in front of his disciples all the time, but this time was different. Jesus put everyone out of the room except for the girl's parents. The reason he did this is clear in the words he said to Jairus when he was told his daughter was dead, "Do not fear, only believe." The Bible shows more than once that unbelief can block miracles.

And they took offense at him. But Jesus said to them, "A prophet is not without honor except in his own town and in his own home." And he did not do many miracles there because of their lack of faith.

Mark 13:57-58

And Jesus rebuked the demon, and it came out of him, and the boy was healed instantly. Then the disciples came to Jesus privately and said, "Why could we not cast it out?" He said to them, "Because of your little faith. For truly, I say to you, if you have faith like a grain of mustard seed, you will say to this mountain, 'Move from here to there,' and it will move, and nothing will be impossible for you.

Matthew 17:18-20

If Jesus was going to perform the miracle, he couldn't have unbelief getting in his way. That is why he put the mourners who laughed at him out of the room. He must have only brought three of the Twelve disciples for the same reason. Their faith was lacking, and so he could not have them with him at this important moment.

There may come a time when you find yourself in the same situation. Not bringing a dead girl back to life, but in a situation where even your friends and vision partners might get in the way because God is telling you to do something that seems impossible, and their faith just isn't there yet. When that time comes, it is good to have confidants, those who you can count on to believe in you and, more importantly, in God to trust his vision for your life when the things you tell them God is going to do don't make any sense.

You will also notice that when Jesus raised the girl, he told her parents not to tell anyone what had happened. That is not the only time Jesus shared a secret with his inner circle. Peter, James, and John were also the only ones present when he was transfigured.

After six days Jesus took with him Peter, James and John the brother of James, and led them up a high mountain by themselves. There he was transfigured before them. His face shone like the sun, and his clothes became as white as

the light. Just then there appeared before them Moses and Elijah, talking with Jesus.

As they were coming down the mountain, Jesus instructed them, "Don't tell anyone what you have seen, until the Son of Man has been raised from the dead."
Matthew 17:1-3, 17:9

Jesus showed his confidants things the world was not ready to see. Your confidants will also be people you can trust to keep your secrets. You might find this hard to believe, but some of the people around you, even those close to you, will get in the way of your purpose if they know everything God has in store for you. I don't just mean your enemies either. There might be trials you know you have to go through, that you're willing to endure for God's sake, which the people who love you will not understand. They will try to protect you from what they believe is danger, because they do not understand God's will for your life.

That is why you have to be careful who you share secrets with. Even if they are the people who will try to block your vision, they might tell someone else, then that person could frustrate your purpose. I don't think I need to tell anyone how quickly information can spread when it starts off as a secret.

The last function of your confidants is arguably the most important. Since you can trust them with your secrets, you can trust them to know your suffering. We see this when Jesus goes to the garden of Gethsemane to pray just a few hours before he is arrested.

They went to a place called Gethsemane, and Jesus said to his disciples, "Sit here while I pray." He took Peter, James and John along with him, and he began to be deeply distressed and troubled. "My soul is overwhelmed with sorrow to the point of death," he said to them. "Stay here and keep watch."

Mark 14:32-34

When Jesus went to pray in Gethsemane, he was so troubled that he felt as if he would die. The scriptures went on to say that as he prayed, he began to sweat blood. It is hard to imagine the kind of stress he was under, knowing the kind of death that awaited him, but most of us know what it is like to feel overwhelmed, and that doesn't stop once you begin operating in your purpose.

You have to remember that God believes in you. He believes in you more than you believe in yourself. He knows your full potential and He will stretch you until you reach it. At times, that stretching is going to be painful. Sometimes you will be stretched to the point where you feel like you are going to break. At those moments, you will be glad that there are people you can talk to.

Any pastor can tell you what it is like to suffer in silence, having to go in front of your congregation and preach every Sunday, while crying on the inside because of the devastating attacks the devil is throwing at you, and feeling like you have to keep it to yourself because you don't want to cause anyone else to slip. You don't want to have that one member who sees what you're going through and says, "If even the pastor is having a hard time fighting this thing, then I don't have a chance" and give up on God. That pressure builds and builds until it can be too much to take. Some pastors explode on their congregations. Some fall back into sin and make the pressure even worse by having something else they have to hide from the people. Sadly, some even commit suicide.

Is that just how it is? No. There is no temptation for which God does not provide a way of escape (1 Corinthians 10:13).

Your confidants are how you escape the pain of silent suffering. They are those to whom you can vent, in front of whom you can be vulnerable. They are the people to whom you can say, "I'm not okay". They will not lose faith because they are spiritually mature enough to know that even someone as close to God as you are can and will still struggle as much as anyone else.

Jesus suffered so we could be saved. Surely, we are no better than Jesus. Sometimes your purpose will involve suffering. You might feel like there's too much to do and not enough time to do it, and so do what Jesus told the seventy-two disciples to do, pray to the Lord of the harvest to send you laborers. You might need someone to hook up with in order to hit the ground running with your purpose, or someone to share ideas with. God will send you Vision Partners to establish that kind of relationship. Then at the worst of times, you will need someone to share your secrets and your suffering with. There's no getting out of suffering, it comes with the territory of fulfilling your God-given purpose. Thanks to your confidants, you will not have to suffer silently.

Notice, however, that I did not say you won't have to suffer alone. That is because, even with laborers, partners, and confidants, your purpose is still *your* purpose. No one can do it for you, and no one will do it with you. Jesus had his seventy-two, his twelve, and his three, but when he went to the cross, he went by himself. Like I said, we are no better than him. When it comes to the vital point where your purpose must be fulfilled, you will go alone.

GO ALONE

When I was growing up, my friends and I used to talk about our college aspirations. It's normal, I think for kids to want to go to college, and to even have some idea about where they want to go, but my friends and I were one-hundred percent sure that one day we would all be Wolverines. We made all kinds of plans for what we would do when we went to the University of Michigan. We practically had our bags packed and we weren't even out of high school yet.

I wish you could have seen how excited I was when I finally got my acceptance letter to U of M. It was literally a dream come true, and I knew it was nothing but God that allowed me to get into the university (but that's a story for another time). I already talked a little about my time at U of M in the earlier chapters of this book, but you might have noticed I never mentioned any of the childhood friends who attended with me. Well, there's a reason for that. None of my friends went to U of M. Everyone had their reasons for not going, some good and some bad. It doesn't really matter why they didn't go, what matters is that I didn't crumple up my acceptance letter and say, "If ya'll not going, then I'm not going."

Not only would that have** been one of the stupidest decisions of my life, it would have been a slap in the face to God who had blessed me to be able to attend one of the top universities in the country. Leaving my friends behind wasn't easy, but I had to face the same fact then that I had to face in various stages of my life: not everyone can go where you're going.

When God calls you, one of the first things he will do is move you out of your comfort zone. That's what He did to Abraham.

The Lord had said to Abram, "Go from your country, your people and your father's household to the land I will show you."

Genesis 12:1

When God told Abraham to leave his family and friends behind, and go off on his own, He wasn't doing it to be mean. Abraham (or Abram, as he was called then) was from Mesopotamia. His people worshipped many false gods. If he had stayed in that environment, or if he had disobeyed God and brought his kindred with him, what do you think the result would have been? I think it would have been the same as when we go to a new place where we don't know anyone, and bring a couple of friends. We just end up hanging around those friends, talking to those friends, and basically doing what we normally do. If Abraham had brought his family along, his people would have concluded that the God talking to him was one of their local deities instead of the one true God. They would have worshipped him with the same pagan rituals and nothing would have changed.

When God calls you out, he doesn't change your environment just for the sake of changing it. He does it because he wants to change your mindset. He wants you to forget everything you thought you knew so that he can begin to teach you to think the way he needs you to think.

It should be noted too, that when I say change your environment, I don't necessarily mean changing your physical environment. God can keep you right where you are and still take you out of your comfort zone. He may remove people from your life by having them drift away, or just be too busy to hang out like they used to. He might give you new responsibilities at work that force you to interact with people you've worked with for years but never really spoke to. However he does it, the first step in setting you up for your purpose is getting you away from the things you're familiar with and forcing you to rely on him.

As I said before, at the end of the day, your purpose is for you and that means not everyone is going to understand what God wants you to do. It isn't just enemies who will try to stop you from doing God's will. Your closest friends, even your confidants, will block you if you let them. No matter how spiritual you are, no one wants to see people they love suffering. Before Jesus went to the cross, he was forced to rebuke Peter for this very reason.

From that time on Jesus began to explain to his disciples that he must go to Jerusalem and suffer many things at the hands of the elders, the chief priests and the teachers of the law, and that he must be killed and on the third day be raised to life. Peter took him aside and began to rebuke him. "Never, Lord!" he said. "This shall never happen to

you!" Jesus turned and said to Peter, "Get behind me, Satan! You are a stumbling block to me; you do not have in mind the concerns of God, but merely human concerns."
Matthew 16:21-23

This passage is deeper than you might think. Yes, Jesus rebukes Peter because he is putting his own love for Jesus before the purposes of God. However, that isn't the most important part. The important part is when Jesus says, "Get behind me, Satan." Satan is the enemy who comes to pull us away from God. Do you know what Satan's primary weapon is for doing that? Temptation. That is why Jesus calls Peter a "stumbling block". Whenever a stumbling block is mentioned in the Bible, it always refers to something that can cause someone to sin.

Jesus never sinned though, you're probably thinking. You're absolutely right. Jesus did not sin, but that doesn't mean Jesus was never *tempted* to sin. We know for a fact that he was tempted by Satan in the desert (Matthew 4:1-11; Luke 4:1-13; Mark 1:12-13). We shouldn't fool ourselves into thinking the devil just gave up after that. Not only was Jesus tempted to sin, but he endured temptation worse than any other human being, because he is the only one who never gave in.

So, when Jesus calls Peter "Satan" and a "stumbling block" he is saying that Peter is tempting him to sin. Namely, he is tempting Jesus to abandon his purpose. Remember, Jesus did not want to go to the cross. It was the reason he was so sorrowful in the garden of Gethsemane. He even asked God if He could find it in His will to allow him to escape his fate (Luke 22:42). With all that on his mind, the last thing Jesus needed right then was for one of his closest friends to try and convince him to not go through with it.

That is why God might even take your confidants away from you. The people who love you the most could become the greatest stumbling blocks when it comes to fulfilling your purpose, because you might be tempted to step away from what God wants you to do, because you know that seeing what you have to go through will be hard on them.

When all is said and done. The only person who can fulfil your purpose is you. Jesus even had someone who was there to carry his cross when he couldn't bear its weight, but even that man could not get on the cross and be crucified for him. There was only one Son of God. It wasn't that Jesus was some random man God chose. The reason God came to Earth in human form was to suffer and die. Jesus was literally the only person who could have done what he did.

You, also, were born for a reason. You are the only one who can do what God needs you to do. That is why God cannot allow anything or anyone to get in the way.

At the same time, even though this entire chapter has been about the fact that you will eventually have to go alone, the truth is you're never *really* alone. Sometimes you will feel alone. Sometimes it will feel like there is no one in the world who understands because, honestly, there isn't. Those lonely times are when you have to remind yourself that God is always with you. He doesn't just see what you are going through. He goes through it with you, because it is He that is working through you to fulfil your purpose (Philippians 2:13).

FINISH THE WORK

I want to begin this final chapter by taking you back in time. It is 67 AD. The apostle Paul is in Rome, the heart of the Roman Empire. He has preached the gospel for decades. His body is battered and scarred with the marks of persecution. He has been beaten, stoned, imprisoned, and ridiculed. Not all of his marks are from persecution though. He has been shipwrecked more than once, and even bitten by a venomous snake.

It wasn't all bad though. He established churches all over the Mediterranean, fearlessly preached the gospel no matter what they did to him. He even managed to bring his message here to Rome, the heart of the empire who worships Caesar as the "son of god". Now, his enemies have finally caught up to him. Paul has been placed under house arrest. Soon he will be executed. Since he is a Roman citizen, he will not be crucified like his Lord. He will die by the sword.

Knowing his death is near, Paul decides to write a letter to his disciple, Timothy. Even though he cannot instruct him in person, he can still give him a couple of final lessons before Timothy is on his own. As he composes the letter we now know as 2 Timothy, he writes the following words:

For I am now ready to be offered, and the time of my departure is at hand. I have fought a good fight, I have finished my course, I have kept the faith: Henceforth there is laid up for me a crown of righteousness, which the Lord, the righteous judge, shall give me at that day: and not to me only, but unto all them also that love his appearing.

2 Timothy 4:6-8

There will come a day when you find yourself reaching the end of your course. You will look back on your life and everything you've done and ask yourself, "Did I do everything I was meant to do in this life? Did I accomplish the mission God gave me when he put me on this planet? Is there a crown of righteousness laid up for me in Heaven?"

Throughout this book, you have learned that God has a purpose for you in life, how to discover that purpose, and what to expect when you are beginning to operate in that purpose. Now, as we come to the end, I just want to encourage you to do one thing: finish the work. Yes, it will be hard at times. There will be times you want to quit, even after you've been operating in your purpose for years. You might feel like you've done enough, and you want to rest. There were times when Paul felt this way.

If I am to live in the flesh, that means fruitful labor for me. Yet which I shall choose I cannot tell. I am hard pressed between the two. My desire is to depart and be with Christ, for that is far better. But to remain in the flesh is more necessary on your account. (Philippians 1:22-24)

The devil will never stop throwing obstacles at you, because the last thing he wants is for you to finish the work God has given you to do, because your purpose is more than just a job God has given you. Your purpose is a part of your design, it is how God works to perfect you, and bring his promises to bear in your life.

When the Bible talks about Jesus's perfection, it says he was obedient even to the death of the cross (Philippians 2:8). We know that Jesus never disobeyed God, but in order to achieve that perfect obedience, it wouldn't have been enough for him to do *almost* everything God wanted him to do. He had to go all the way. That is why, as he died on the cross, Jesus was able to say, "It is finished" (John 19:30).

There is another story in the Bible, when God tells Abraham to sacrifice his son, Isaac. This is after God has already promised to make Abraham a father of many nations, and that it was all supposed to start with Isaac.

Then the word of the Lord came to him: "This man will not be your heir, but a son who is your own flesh and blood will be your heir." He took him outside and said, "Look up at the sky and count the stars—if indeed you can count them." Then he said to him, "So shall your offspring be." Abram believed the Lord, and he credited it to him as righteousness.

Genesis 15:4-5

Abraham, because of his unshakable faith in God, obeyed the command that was given to him. Fortunately, an angel stopped him at the last second. After the angel stopped him, God said this:

"I swear by myself, declares the Lord, that because you have done this and have not withheld your son, your only son, I will surely bless you and make your descendants as numerous as the stars in the sky and as the sand on the seashore. Your descendants will take possession of the cities of their enemies, and through your offspring all nations on earth will be blessed, because you have obeyed me." (Genesis 22:16-18)

He repeated the promise he had made to Abraham before Isaac was even born. Abraham had believed God when he made the promise, but it is easy to believe in the promises of God when you're staring up at the stars. Could Abraham continue to believe in that promise when God told him to kill the son He had promised to him? If Abraham had refused to sacrifice Isaac because Isaac was the only way his purpose could be fulfilled, that would mean his faith had a limit and God could not use him. But Abraham had enough faith to go all the way to the end, believing God even when it didn't seem to make any sense. Only when Abraham had been pushed to the brink could God fulfil his purposes in Abraham.

You will also be pushed to the brink, to some point where you feel as if you can go no further, or like what God is telling you doesn't make sense. When that happens, keep the faith. God began a good work in you, and he will see it through to the end. You will begin to see the manifestation of God's plan for your life and, in the end, there will be a crown of righteousness waiting for you in Heaven. In that moment, all of the struggles you endured will turn to glory, as you look upon the face of God and He says, "Well done, good and faithful servant." Then you will understand that your purpose was always greater than your tears.

DEDICATION

I would like to dedicate this book to the memory of my late grandfather, Ennis Bryant. Ennis Bryant believed in me and my purpose before I was even born. My mom was pregnant with me at the age of 19 and she had a bright future ahead of her. My family was pushing for her to go to New York and have an abortion. Ennis took a stand and told my mother that the baby she was carrying was going to be a leader and he said that he was going to do whatever he had to do to help in raising this child.

My grandfather knew I was going to be a leader and I was going to be something special. He already knew I had purpose. My grandfather taught me a lot of things and always bought me McDonald's. I remember doing a small radio show in the living room where we would record our voices on a tape-recorder like we were reporting the news.

My grandfather taught me to never co-sign for people and always save my money. He always had multiple vehicles and didn't lack for anything; maybe that is where I get that from.

I have had the opportunity to lead so many people to Christ. It gives me great joy to introduce people to Jesus whether friend or even a complete stranger. I have to admit that my fondest time of introducing someone to Jesus is when I had to see my grandfather laying in the hospital dealing with an ailment that had attacked his body.

I got the call that my grandfather was not doing well and I needed to get to the hospital. I immediately began to pray and say to God that I had given up a lot of things in life to serve Him and I didn't say that He owed me, but I told God that I just needed his help. I asked God to give me time to get to the hospital to minister to my grandfather. I arrived at the hospital and my grandfather was still around. After the formalities, I led my grandfather to Jesus. My granddad had been going to church from time to time but his relationship with Jesus was not where it needed to be. My granddad gave me a chance at life, I had to make sure that he had a chance at eternal life with Jesus.

It was my honor to do my granddad's eulogy at his home-going celebration. My granddad spoke purpose on my life and I dedicate this book to him to honor his memory.

www.ingramcontent.com/pod-product-compliance
Lightning Source LLC
Chambersburg PA
CBHW070812050426
42452CB00011B/2006